WITHDRAWN

When
Dinosaurs Ruled

Library Edition Published 1990

Published by Marshall Cavendish Corporation
147 West Merrick Road
Freeport, Long Island
N.Y. 11520

Printed in Hong Kong by Colorcraft Ltd.

All rights reserved. No part of this book may be reproduced or utilized in any form or by any means electronic or mechanical, including photocopying, recording, or by an information storage and retrieval system, without permission from the copyright holders.

© Marshall Cavendish Limited 1990
© Cherrytree Press Ltd 1988

Designed and produced by
AS Publishing

Library of Congress Cataloging-in-Publication Data

Head, John G. (John Gerald)
    When dinosaurs ruled / written by John G. Head : illustrated by Bernard Robinson.
        p. cm. — (Ages of the Earth)
    "First published 1988 by Cherrytree Press Ltd."- T.p. verso.
    Summary: On their Space-Time Shuttle tour of the prehistoric world, a brother and sister land in the Jurrasic Period where they see the largest and most ferocious land animals that have ever lived.
    ISBN 1-85435-186-9 ISBN 1-85435-182-6 (set)
    1. Dinosaurs — Juvenile literature. [1. Dinosaurs. 2. Prehistoric animals.] I. Robinson, Bernard, 1930- ill. II. Title. III. Series: Head, John G. (John Gerald). Ages of the earth.
    QE862.D5H52 1989
    567.9' 1-dc20   89-7326
                                                                  CIP
                                                                   AC

AGES OF THE EARTH

When Dinosaurs Ruled

John G. Head

Illustrated by Bernard Robinson

MARSHALL CAVENDISH
NEW YORK · LONDON · TORONTO · SYDNEY

PUBLIC LIBRARY
CEDAR RAPIDS, IOWA 52401

It was the ninth day of the trip. Mike and his sister Helen were on a Space-Time Shuttle tour of the prehistoric world. During the previous week, they had traveled 600 million years back in time to start their explorations in the Cambrian period. From there, they had moved on to visit the Ordovician, Silurian, Devonian, Carboniferous, and Permian periods. They had seen all kinds of living prehistoric animals. The previous day, they had landed in the Triassic Period – and seen their first dinosaurs.

Today, they were in the Jurassic Period. With luck, they would see some of the largest and most ferocious land animals that have ever lived.

Timcom, the on-board computer, had pinpointed the best
place on Earth to land. Now they were waiting. Helen was
pretending not to be interested, but Bob, the captain; Atty, his
second-in-command; and Jenny, the Space-Time Ranger, were
all glued to the Shuttle windows.

   "Please, can we go out," pleaded Mike.
   "Let's see what's out there first," said Bob. "There may be
some really dangerous animals around, and good will and a
stun gun will not protect you."

Mike had won the trip as a prize for coming first in a contest for
children from all over the world. Bob and the others were eager
that he particularly should see as much as possible; but the risk
was too great. Mike sulked.

Outside, nothing moved except the trees swaying in the breeze.
Then, they heard a noise, a long shrieking sound; and a huge
shadow fell across the window. More shrieks followed, and
more strange shadows appeared on the ground.

"Look up, not down," said Timcom. They all craned their
necks, but they could not see the creatures that were swooping
around the Shuttle. They were flying reptiles, pterosaurs with
bat-like wings.

At last, one of the creatures swooped low enough for them to
get a good look.

"See how flimsy it is," said Jenny. "It's so light the wind is blowing it around like a kite."

"It's a Rhamphorhynchus," said Timcom. "It is one of the smaller pterosaurs. Some of the later species had wings as big as the Shuttle's."

After they had investigated the Shuttle, the pterosaurs glided away. There was nothing else to see, so Jenny suggested that they followed them. Bob put the craft into its hover mode, and at a distance, they skimmed along behind the reptiles. They followed them all the way to the shore of a huge sea and over the surface of the water.

The pterosaurs drifted on the wind and swooped down every so
often to pick a fish from the waves. They were fascinating to
watch – but not when you were supposed to be on a dinosaur
safari.

"Let's go back to the land," said Mike. "I want to see some
real animals." He had not spotted the bulky shapes on the
distant shore.

"Look, Mike," shouted Helen. "Look at those fellows."

"Those are Diplodoci. They are dinosaurs belonging to the
group called sauropods. Diplodocus was not the biggest, but it
was the longest," said Timcom.

"Please, let's go and see them," pleaded Mike.

9

Captain Marsh had other ideas.

"Sorry, Mike," he said. "But while we are over the sea, we might as well take a look beneath the waves. Those sauropods can wait for a bit. So, fasten your seat belts." With that, he altered the Shuttle's mode and direction, and they dived slowly into the sea.

The Shuttle suddenly lurched as if it had been batted. It had been batted, by the tail of a great sea lizard. It was a plesiosaur, which was thrashing about in the water, trying to eat this solid new creature that had appeared in its territory. Only when it gave up the effort and swam away could they see it clearly. It had huge paddles like wings, and it looked as if it

were flying through the water. Bob decided not to follow it. His passengers were all feeling green and shaky. So they parked the Shuttle on the sea bed and watched the fishes.

"Aren't those huge curly things amazing," said Helen, who loved exploring underwater. "What are they, Timcom?"

"Those are ammonites," said Mike. "I found a fossil of one once. It's in the school museum."

"That's right," said Timcom. "Ammonites were mollusks, related to the nautiloids that you saw in the Ordovician sea, and to octopuses in your own time. There were many different kinds of them in the Jurassic and Cretaceous seas, but then they became extinct – like the dinosaurs."

Plesiosaur

"I expect dinosaurs will be extinct before we get to see any of them," said Mike.

"Okay, hint taken," said Bob. "Let's go back up and find a Brontosaurus."

"Apatosaurus," interrupted Timcom. "Brontosaurus is an outmoded name for the sauropod to which you refer."

"Oh, do shut up," muttered Helen.

Bob landed the Shuttle where they had seen the Diplodocus. But the place was deserted.

"Now we've missed our only opportunity," fumed Mike.

"Don't be rude," said Atty, "or we'll leave you behind when we go for our walk."

Mike was like a dog when he heard the word "walk." If he'd had a tail, he would have wagged it. He raced to get into his lesion-proof suit. When they were all ready, Bob, who was staying behind, gave them strict instructions to go no farther than half a mile from the Shuttle, and to stick together. Atty was carrying the most powerful stun-gun ever invented. They were all a bit scared.

They need not have worried. All they found were footprints.
Mind you, they were quite some footprints. Mike and Helen
were almost up to their waists when they stood in them. They
followed the footprints as far as they could, but then Timcom
told them over the intercom that it was time to come back.
Mike sulked all the way. He sulked even more when he saw
what Bob had been watching while they were gone. It was a
baby Brontosaurus (sorry Timcom, a baby Apatosaurus!) with
an older one.

Brontosaurus
(Apatosaurus)

"Timcom really has found us a perfect
spot," said Bob. "We are obviously
parked just by the route these creatures
follow to the forest where they feed.
You can see it in the distance. We'll
go there after lunch."

Mike had never felt less hungry. Why
couldn't they go now? They ate quickly,
(not that a meal squeezed from tubes
ever took long), and then smoothly
glided to a spot closer to the forest.
Thanks to a lot of nagging from Mike, Bob
agreed that they would all go out on foot.
Timcom's remote camera would keep a
watchful eye on them and warn of any danger.

But the scene they saw when they reached
the forest was a peaceful one, and it was
really spectacular. A whole herd of
Brontosauruses!
    "I hope Timcom is getting good pictures
of this," said Jenny. "What is that
striped thing over there?"
    "That is a Camptosaurus," said Timcom,
"and I have made an adequate record of it."
    In addition to the Camptosaurus, there
were birds in the trees and some little furry
mammals. It was a wonderful sight.

Robinson

Archaeopteryx

"That looks more like a little dinosaur than a real bird,"
said Mike peering up into the branches.

"That is an Archaeopteryx," said Timcom. "It's the oldest
bird fossil known, but many scientists dispute that the creature
was a bird. Some think that it was a dinosaur."

"Well, which is it?" asked Mike.

"I'm not a human," said Timcom. "I can't tell you."

"Well, I'm not a computer," said Jenny, "so I can't be sure,
but they look like a bird's feathers to me."

"It's got very scaly legs, like a lizard," said Helen.

"I'm going to climb up and get a better look," said Mike.
But at his first move toward the tree, the Archaeopteryx took to
flight.

"That's birdlike enough for me," said Bob.

16

"Keep very still, Mike," whispered Helen. "You've scared off the bird. Don't scare this sweet little thing away." She was looking at a little mammal. It was so tame that she was able to pick it up and stroke it – not that she could feel its fur through her suit. Mike immediately started to take his suit off, but the others stopped him.

"We don't want you carrying prehistoric fleas back to the 20th Century AD," laughed Atty.

"There is no fossil evidence that fleas existed in the Jurassic Period," intoned Timcom, but as usual, nobody took much notice.

Nobody was taking much notice of anything but the little creature in Helen's arms. They hadn't seen the great big beast that had lumbered up to them.

They heard the creature before they saw it. It was a
Brontosaurus – a young one – and it was whining.

"That's the one we saw before, this morning," cried Mike.
"It's limping. It must be hurt. It's in pain."

"If it's hurt, something must have hurt it," said Bob. "Back
to the Shuttle, everyone!"

Mike took no notice of the Captain. As the others headed for
safety, Mike set off after the Brontosaurus, followed by Bob. He
was furious.

"Come back here immediately," Bob bellowed. But it was
too late. The bellow that Mike heard was a far louder one. It
came from an Allosaurus, a monster thirty feet tall, with huge
legs that pounded after Mike and the fleeing dinosaur.

Mike ran as fast as he could, but the creature reached him in moments. Bob fired his stun-gun. It was only a small one, not like the powerful one that Atty had. Atty and the girls had almost reached the Shuttle. They were much too far away to help. They had heard the monstrous roaring and the pounding feet. Now they just stood, frozen with fear, too scared even to look.

Allosaurus

The stun-gun hit its target. As the creature's clawed foot struck out toward the boy, Mike dropped to the ground and lay still.

The Allosaurus stopped and looked. Bob closed his eyes and prayed. When he opened them, the dinosaur had lost interest in the seemingly dead creature on the ground. It liked its meat live, and it had the smell of blood in its nostrils.

Mike's paralyzed body lay where it was. Yards away, the Allosaurus closed on the exhausted sauropod. Its savage claws lashed the animal's hide, making a huge, bloody gash in its side. Screaming with pain, the sauropod crashed to the ground, its neck thrashing wildly. Then, the Allosaurus severed the neck with one bite from its huge jaws. The Brontosaurus was dead.

Mike was alive. Bob waited cautiously. One movement from him, or from Mike returning to consciousness, might attract the creature's attention. He had to rescue Mike while the great carnivore was occupied with its meal. Carefully, on his stomach, he edged toward the little figure. He was within twenty yards of him when Mike came to.

"What are you doing down there, Bob?" he said, scrambling loudly to his feet. Bob froze once again. So did the Allosaurus.

It lifted its great head and turned its eyes on this dead creature that had come alive. It decided to investigate and strode toward Mike, who by now had remembered only too well where he was.

This time, it was the Allosaurus's turn for a shock. Unknown to Bob, Atty had been silently edging along behind him with the laser-stunner. One blast from it, and the Allosaurus slumped to the ground. Bob raced forward, grabbed Mike who was too weak to run, and carried him back to the Shuttle.

"He'll be out for at least half an hour,"said Atty, motioning back to the Allosaurus. "Quite something, wasn't he! I don't suppose anyone will ever be allowed to leave a vehicle during the Jurassic again, after that."

"Yes," said Bob. "I shouldn't have allowed it to happen. It was my fault."

"Oh, but it was such a wonderful adventure!" said Mike.

"You wouldn't have thought so if you'd seen that beast ripping your sauropod friend to bits. Besides, it could have been you," said Bob.

Jenny and Helen had seen everything on Timcom's holoscreen. They had been absolutely terrified.

"Especially the first time," said Helen, "when you missed the Allosaurus and hit Mike instead."

"I wasn't aiming at the Allosaurus." said Bob. "Stunning Mike and stopping him from running was his only chance. The gun I had would have had no effect on a raging three-ton menace like that."

"He doesn't look quite so fierce now," said Jenny, "though he'll be really mad when he wakes up. He's losing all his supper." The Allosaurus's supper was being enjoyed by a whole flock of pterosaurs, who had flown down like vultures to eat the leftovers.

Mike felt a bit groggy after his ordeal and decided to go to bed soon after supper. Bob was still upset at his own stupidity in exposing them all to such danger. Even though they were not moving on in time, he decided to put the craft into Earth orbit while they slept instead of leaving it on the ground. He wasn't taking any chances.

There was no question of anyone leaving the Shuttle the next day, and not a murmur of complaint. Atty parked the craft in open country by an outcrop of almost bare rock. Timcom surveyed the scene, but there was nothing of interest except a few clumps of trees. It was hot outside, and nothing stirred except for the pterosaurs that once again had wheeled down to take a look at them.

Then, a bleep on Timcom's screen sent them rushing to the window. A Stegosaurus had been sleeping at the foot of the cliff. It was so huge and jagged in shape that not even the

Ornitholestes

cameras had spotted it among the rocks. Now, it rose to its feet
and plodded toward a clump of ferns.

As it did, another creature scrambled down the rock face and
scampered after it. It was an Ornitholestes, a nimble, vicious
little carnivore. It danced around the big dinosaur, nipping at
its sides and feet. The Stegosaurus took no notice for a while.
Then, suddenly, it swung its tail. One of the great spikes struck
the little carnivore's thin leg and almost broke it. The
Ornitholestes limped away, and the Stegosaurus went on
munching the ferns.

   "It's amazing!" said Helen. "Look at those spikes. No
wonder that little dinosaur got out of the way. And look at
those great things on its back.
What are they for?"

Stegosaurus

"Well," said Jenny, before Timcom could answer, "I think they act as armor and as radiators. He can probably stand sideways to the sun to get warm and head-on to get cool – like the sail-backed reptiles we saw in the Permian."

"Why is he by himself?" asked Mike. "I thought you said that plant-eaters like him lived in herds."

"If we keep track of him," said Jenny, "he'll probably lead us to his herd."

They spent almost the whole afternoon watching the Stegosaurus. It was several hours before the herd came into view. The animals looked as if they had been to a water hole. Some of them were caked with mud.

"You can see now," said Timcom, "that the individual Stegosaurus you have been watching its quite an old specimen. The hide is dull in color and pockmarked. But the animal is large enough to have been the leader of the herd."

By now, the old Stegosaurus was mingling with the others. But he did not stay with them for long. A younger male confronted him, striking the ground with its tail. The older animal backed off, and the younger one led the herd away to graze. Then, once more, he turned his attention on the old male. He galloped toward him and struck as hard as he could. The old male fought back hard, tossing the younger one against the jagged plates on its back. But he could not keep up the fight for long. In the end, he dropped to his knees. The battle was over. The old male was on his own for good. The young one would lead the herd from now on.

"That was horrible," said Mike.

"It's a good thing you are not out there, or you'd be trying to bind its wounds," said Atty.

"What will happen to him?" asked Mike, as he watched the old animal stagger back to its rocky hideaway.

"He'll be all right for a while," said Jenny. "He's a tough guy. His wounds will heal, and there's plenty of food for him. He'll be okay until he gets really slow. Then, even that little Ornitholestes will be able to finish him off."

"If one of those Allosauruses came along right now, I wouldn't bet on his chances," said Atty.

By now, the sun was going down. It was time to take off again and move on to the Cretaceous Period.

"Not yet, please," said Mike.

"Why?" asked Jenny. "Haven't you seen enough today? There will be plenty to see tomorrow. We may even meet a Tyrannosaurus."

"Just a bit longer, please," begged Mike.

"All right," said Bob. "We'll stay until dark."

They did not have to wait until dark, because Mike's great wish was granted there and then. It was to see a Brachiosaurus, the biggest land animal that ever lived. The vast sauropod came alongside the Shuttle, and the ground seemed to shake as the gigantic creature stomped by.

"He must be 25 yards long," gasped Atty.

"Isn't he magnificent!" said Bob. "I'm glad we spoil you so much, Mike. I wouldn't have missed seeing him for all the other animals put together!"

Brachiosaurus

AGES OF THE EARTH TOUR

Shuttle back in time and see with your own eyes 600 million years of Earth's history in just three weeks.

Periods	Years Ago (Millions)	Plants and Animals
Pre-cambrian	4,500	No life on Earth to start with. Tiny plants appear about 3,000 million years ago in the sea; first known animals appear about 700 million years ago.
Cambrian	600	No life on land, but in the sea there are creatures called graptolites and trilobites, corals and sponges, shellfish and jellyfish.
Ordovician	500	More graptolites and trilobites in sea. Creatures called brachiopods, and the first fish — which have armor.
Silurian	440	Land plants appear. Lots of fish in the sea and giant sea-scorpions.
Devonian	395	The age of fishes. Sea teems with all kinds, including huge jawed fish and sharks. Small creatures leave the sea to live on land. Amphibians evolve from fish.
Carboniferous	345	Giant land plants in coal swamps. Large amphibians and the first insects, including some giants. Reptiles evolve from amphibians.
Permian	280	Lots more reptiles and fewer amphibians. Trilobites die out.

PALEOZOIC ERA

AGES OF THE EARTH TOUR

Visit each of these periods and see the animals and plants of bygone ages, monsters of land and sea and sky.

	Periods	Years Ago (Millions)	Plants and Animals
MESOZOIC ERA	**Triassic**	225	The first dinosaurs. Large reptiles and shelled creatures called ammonites in the sea. Mammals evolve from reptiles.
	Jurassic	200	Lots of dinosaurs, including huge sauropods and carnosaurs. Pterosaurs in the air. Birds evolve from reptiles.
	Cretaceous	135	New kinds of dinosaurs, including ones with armor. Small mammals and birds. First flowering plants. At the end of the period, dinosaurs and many other creatures die out.
CENOZOIC ERA	**Tertiary**	65	The age of mammals. Many kinds of mammals evolve, including horses, elephants, and apes. Coniferous forests and grasslands.
	Quaternary	2	Mammoths, wooly mammoths and saber-toothed cats live through Ice Ages. Ancestors of humans appear. The first humans appear.

Index